DOWN-HOME

DOWN-HOME

MONOLOGUES IN THE LANGUAGE
OF
RURAL AMERICA

ROGER KARSHNER

Dramaline Publications

Dramaline Publications
36-851 Palm View Road
Rancho Mirage, CA 92270
Phone 619/770-6076 Fax 619/770-4507

Cover by John Sabel

This book is printed on 55# Glatfelter acid-free paper. A a paper that meets the requirements of the American Standard of Permanence of paper for printed library material.

CONTENTS

Womenfolk

Menfolk

INTRODUCTION

The speeches in this book are based on my recollections of people in Ross County, Ohio.

Ross County, Ohio, is located in the south-central part of the state, roughly between Columbus and Cincinnati. It's a nice hunk of country with gentle rolling hills and some of the best farmland in the nation. I have fond recollections of it, its easy-living ways, its quietness, and regal solitude. It was a wonderful place for a kid to know.

But the thing I remember best about Ross County is its people; those good, hard-working people, neat as pins, honest, respectful of the land and each other; people who were kind and gentle in their ways of living. Perhaps many of them weren't worldly, no. But there are things more important than knowing that the salad fork goes to the left. These Ross County people knew about common sense; they knew about hunkering down and hanging in; they knew how to shoulder responsibility; they knew that a husband and wife devoted meant children growing up without insecurity and fear; they knew about peace coming from the acceptance of simple truths; they knew how to deal gracefully with life's vicissitudes because they courageously faced the capriciousness of the seasons from dawn to dusk throughout their down-home lives.

Bless their ever lovin' hearts.

RK

WOMENFOLK

CHARACTER MAKES THE MAN

Ada and Will Plue ran Shady Corners Tavern in Adelphi, Ohio. Like its name, it was on a corner; unlike is name, it wasn't shady. It was an exposed, rectangular, slummy joint of low-slung obtuseness, insinuating itself trashily into the Christian neatness of surrounding homes. It was an eyesore. But, despite its delapidation, its rusted-out sign swinging above its entrance, it was a magnetizing hotspot attracting good-timers from Adelphi and nearby towns. Ada and Will put together didn't quite make a person. They were that skinny. A result, perhaps, of a lifetime diet of Chesterfields and Miller High Life beer. But they were real interesting characters; warm, caring, and voluntary of time and pocketbook. Especially Ada, whose smile was wider than she was, whose dresses hung on her like moss from sticks, whose expletives could crack plaster. Not religious, and eschewed by those who were, I always suspected that profane-mouthed, pipecleaner-boned little Ada had more compassion in the tip of her spikey nose than the combined congregations of Ross County churches. And she loved her Will.

Here she speaks of how they met:

ADA PLUE

I first met Will the night 'e come up from Charleston. He'd been drivin' all night long an' 'e looked like the slum side a hell, 'e did, that crazy sonofabitch. Looked 'bout the same as 'e does t'day—a real skinny bastard with no teeth. But 'e was sure cute. Least ways, I sure thought 'e was. He had this here way about 'im. Man could charm the livin' daylights outta a woman. Still can.

Anyway, he sure as the devil got through t' me, gums an' all. A woman don't notice the uglies on a man when he's got himself some character, when 'e's got a holt on soul an' can spill it out an' show it an' let it take over ever'thin' around 'im, when 'e's got it big and huge.

Well, sir, it was a rainy night, I 'member, a-kind a drizzlin' behind a bone-cold wind. I was settin' here, settin' here right at this very table, was settin' here doin' some serious work on a double Southern Comfort when Will slid in, a-lookin' like a ruptured pup. His car had busted on 'im up near Floyd Mears' place, an' the crazy bastard'd walked all the way in. He went on over t' the bar there an' ordered a shot, an' 'e looked real interestin' standin' there in the light from the Miller's sign. That there red neon on that crazy sideways face a his was just like sunrise on Mount Rushmore—it lit 'im up t' real advantage, it did. Anyway, he looked real okay t' me. I've always liked men who look like they bin in constant pain fer a few days.

He couldn't help a-noticin' me a-settin' here with m' mind in 'is pants, so he come on over an' set down an' bought me another double Comfort. An' we started in a-talkin', him an' me; a-talkin', and a-spinnin' a little history an' a lot a lies an' gettin' real chummy. After awhile, I felt m'self a-driftin' inta 'is slow-freight charm. I say slow-freight 'cause 'e was a-comin' at me steady with a heavy load.

Well, that night started up the beginnin' of it. An' me an' Will's been a-talkin' real chummy like ever since. An' ya know, I still git a ticklin' in m' butt when I see that there beat-up skinny bastard comin' at me from 'cross a room.

PINBALL

During my time in Hallsville, the most apocalyptic event was the discovery that a pinball machine had been moved into the ice cream store. The outcries of the pious and the self-righteous echoed across the county, and the terrible swift sword of the fearful few was swung in great verbal arcs, stirring in many a breast hatred for that "demon machine among us."

Sophie Claybaugh was at the vanguard of the battle for the summary removal of this dastardly device. Seemingly demure, sweet, gentle little Sophie leapt into the breach with fiery-eyed fervor when this "demon among us" reared its menacing, devilish, electronic, nickel-grabbing head.

SOPHIE CLAYBAUGH

It's gotta go! It's gotta go, I'm a tellin' ya! That there Lucifer's device has gotta go!

There's no place fer a devil's machine in a Christian community like this here. We got us standards to keep. We got us kiddies t' raise clean an' pure in the shadow o' the cross! We don't act now, that there machine's gonna be the ruination of this here fine little place. We don't do somethin' right away, God only knows what's a-gonna follow: gamblin', bettin', playin' the horses. God only knows! Once't the devil gits a foothold, he don't easy let go. Once't he gets 'is horns in the youth a this here community, once't they git the feel fer 'im, well . . . then that's gonna be the end a peace an' security in our little town!

From little acorns mighty chestnuts grow. First pinball, then— *beer!* Then, heaven forbid—*a wet county!* Then, 'fore ya know it— *fast women!* Then good-time men a-comin' on down here from Columbus lookin' fer a wild time. No tellin' just where it'll lead to. An' think a yer youth, those fresh little blossoms on the tree a life. Think a 'em. Think a 'em a-hangin' 'round down at that there ice cream store a-pumpin' ever nickel inta that there machine, spendin' their school money, money that should be a-goin' fer books an' education, money they could be savin' up an' droppin' inta the collection plate of a Sunday as a way a helpin' the work a the Lord.

We gotta git that there pinball out now while the gittin's good! That there devil's machine with all them evil lights an' bells an' funny little demon balls! Damnation! Jesus drove the gamblers outta the temple. Now we gotta drive that there pinball outta Ross County. We gotta rise up an' take holt before it's two machines an' then three and then . . . then who knows how many. The whole derned county'll be wall-t'-wall with slot machines an' pinballs an' sin! We gotta take up the Almighty sword an' cut out the cancer among us while the cuttin's good.

Praise the Lord!

SHAKE HANDS WITH YOUR FELLOW MAN

Old Anna Beal was Old Anna Beal for as far back as I can remember. Even when she was a relatively young woman. Some people are like that. Old before their time in speech, attitude, and mannerisms. In Anna Beal's case, I have a feeling she'd been old since birth.

Anna, and her husband, Norvel, ran a big farm, had prospered, had raised seven children, and (so far as anybody knew) had never been outside Ross County. For the Beals, even a trip into Chillicothe, the county seat thirteen miles distant, was a long and arduous adventure that they prepared for well in advance by studying maps, prepping their old Chrysler, and reconnoitering. Not only were the Beals greatly apprehensive regarding travel, they were also philosophically dead-set against it, believing it frivolous, soul-shriveling and downright idiotic.

OLD ANNA BEAL

Was born right here, plan t' die here. Don't need t' be a-trav'lin' 'round like some eedyot. Not a dern thing on the other side a the fence that inter'sts me one iota. Got ever'thin' I need right here. Got m' husband, the kiddies, m' family, an' friends. What else is there, anyway? Trav'lin'? Pshaw!

Some people, they gotta be a-movin' 'round all the time, jumpin' 'round like a bullfrog in heat from one lily pad t' other, livin' outta a suitcase, warshin' out their underwear in some hotel sink somewhere. Ain't no way fer a person t' live. Like Dewey an' Jessie, they're like that. Always runnin' off someplace ever' whipstitch a-snappin' pictures a stuff with their Brownie. They gotta whole bunch a albums full a junk: pictures a Lake Erie, the Ohio Caverns, the Warshington Monument, the Procter an' Gamble plant down at Cincinnata. Why, they even got pictures a the desert. The desert! Drivin' all the way out t' California t' take pictures of a bunch a sand. Can ya imagine? If I wanna look at sand, I'll just drive on over t' Snyder's gravel pit.

Crazy how some people gotta be a-runnin' all over the place lookin' at stuff that ain't gonna do 'em one bit a good. Waste a time, if ya ask me.

Heard some person er other say one time that trav'lin' broadens ya. Well, I don't believe it. Way I figure it, it actually narras a person. Only thing it broadens is yer rear end. I figure the real important things in this here life is right under yer nose just fer the lookin'. But heck, most people either can't see 'em er just ain't got the gumption t' look. Look around ya right now. All kinds a beauty. All kinds a wonderful, interestin' people. An' how many of us ever git t' know anythin' about 'em? What's the last time ya reached over and tapped yer neighbor on the shoulder an' said, "Hi there, friend, shake hands with yer fella man?" Make ya a bet right now. Bet ya never have.

It takes a special person t' see what's under 'is nose, t' git a handle on what's around 'im. You learn t' do that an' you'll have a good life and you'll save yerself a bundle on train fare.

I got me ever'thin' right here I could ever want. Got the kiddies, got Norvel. He's a wonderful man, Norvel. Stands right behind me, never wavers.

Yep, I got it by the tail, I have. Got it good an' got it simple. I'm a livin' the good life. I don't have to go nowhere. I got it all right here.

TWO LITTLE DEVILS

Martha Mae Hartman's husband was a drummer and was out on the road a lot. While he was away, Martha Mae tended their spotless, two-by-four little place near Salt Creek and engaged in a pastime that she undertook with willing glee—gossiping. Whether on the phone or huddling with the girls at the Ladies' Aid or Methodist Church, Martha Mae involved herself wholeheartedly with the latest, juiciest, raciest information regarding the locals. She couldn't resist passing along a hot tidbit. And she was a notorious crepe-hanger, too; especially fond of a story with a trace of the macabre, a hint of gore, a glint of gristle to which she would add the chilling, hyperbolic, Martha Mae Hartman touch.

MARTHA MAE HARTMAN

Them two was always inta somethin' er other, always up ta some kinda mischief. What one of 'em didn't think of, the other one did. Two little devils. I always tole people, "Them two is gonna git in over their heads one a these days, you mark m' words." You 'member how they was. Always scarin' up trouble. Like the time one Halloween when they pushed a manure spreader down Bainbridge Hill and it got away from 'em an' took off lickety-split and busted through the church right inta a prayer meetin'. Throwed manure from one end a the place t' the other. The Church never smelled right after that, either. Them little devils. And then there was the time they jimmied the wheels on Ralph Crumwell's hearse and it busted and Earl Delong's casket came a flyin' out the back of it right inta the family car. An awful mess. Them two little devils.

I mean, it's awful what happened to 'em an' all, but what ya expect? The way they was a-goin', they couldn't a wound up no differ'nt. Besides, any derned fool knows how dangerous it is t' go flyin' a kite from a wire. But not them two. An' a-flyin' it on a Sund'y, too. Lordy. The little heathens. Out there a-flyin' a kite on a Sund'y. And a-flyin' it in the cemet'ry, too, walkin' over the graves just a big as ya please with a kite on a wire, a-climbin' up on gravestones and such. Disgraceful.

Understand when that there wire hit that high-tension cable, the electric blew 'em right outa their shoes, and they lit up just like a couple a chest X-rays. An' then steam started a-rollin' off 'em and then . . . powie! their eyeballs blew right outta their sockets!

I went over t' the funeral home to pay my respects. It was a closed-casket affair, but Ralph Crumwell let me take a peek at 'em. Why, you wouldn't a believed it. Burned to a crisp, they was. Looked like a couple a potata chips. Fierce.

I knew it. I kept tellin' people them two was headed fer big trouble. Little devils.

S-E-X

We had our share of spinsters in Hallsville, but Jessie P. (for Pritchard) was the epitome of virginity. Jessie P. was a big woman with a lineless, pretty, forgiving face who loved the color lavender, which she always wore and it had, therefore, become her azure trademark. Jessie P. lived alone in a small brick house behind the dairy where she took in sewing jobs, did chair caning, and intricate needlepoint. Rumor had it that Jessie P. had been quite a looker in her day and had had many beaus but had maintained her chastity and had drifted into spinsterhood due to an ingrained fundamentalist attitude regarding the luciferian aspects of S-E-X.

JESSIE P. (FOR PRITCHARD)

I never did find the right man. Bunch a losers, men. All of 'em got the same thing on their mind . . . *(She spells it.)* S-E-X.

But I had m' share a beaus, though. Believe it er not, I was pretty dern spiffy when I was young. I cut a real rusty, I did. Fact is, I even went with this here shoe salesman fer close t' fifteen years. An' he knew know t' keep 'is place, too, I saw t' that. Not that 'e always wanted to, now mind ya, no siree Bob. More'n once he got a little handsy, a little rover-through-the-clover. Jus' like all men . . . (*She spells it.)* S-E-X.

He used t' come over ever' Thursd'y an' Sund'y nights, an' 'e always brought along a nice present a some kind—like toilet water, stationery, peanut brittle, er something like that. An' he took care a the whole fam'ly when it came t' shoes, too, outfitted the whole bunch of us from samples. But underneath, he was jus' like all men, same ole story . . . *(She spells it.)* S-E-X.

But I always told 'im, "Foster," Foster Thurston, that was 'is name. "Foster," I'd say, "The Good Lord doesn't intend the fruit t' be eaten before it gets picked." But he never gave up, that devil. An' sometimes, as much as I hate t' admit it, I had a hard time a-keepin' the fruit on the tree.

He even proposed t' me once, gave me a ring an' ever'thing. A big diamond. No chip, I'll tell ya. Daddy had it appraised over at Meyers' jewelry store in Chillicothe, an' it was the real McCoy—blue-white an' nearly a quarter carat. An' the set didn't leave any green mark or anything. But after he gave me that ring, he started gettin' awful pushy.

Then, one night, while he was slippin' a sample oxford on m' foot, he ran his hand all the way up my stocking. Gave me the funniest feeling. Never felt anything like it before or since. Was like this twinge all over. An' I knew right away what that feeling was; it was the presence of the devil, the presence of Satan himself right there inside m' petticoat.

Well, that there indecency was jus' too much for m' Christian sensibilities t' handle. So, I told that there handsome shoe salesman to get up and get on out a m' life. Was a hard thing t' do. An' unscrewin' that beautiful blue-white diamond ring from m' finger dern near broke m' heart. But, lemme ask ya, what else could a girl do under such circumstances?

An' ya know what? I've never found any other man no different. All the same. All got that there . . . *(She spells it.)* S-E-X business in their heads, all lookin' fer some easy woman.

Every now an' then, though, I have t' admit it, I do think about that there shoe hustler, wonder where 'e's parkin' 'is sample case. But, what the heck, men aren't everything, there's other things in this here life bigger'n runnin' 'round with a fire in yer britches. So men, I've jus' learned t' put 'em outta m' mind. Don't need 'em. I jus' keep m' mind on the straight and narra.

A MESSA SQUIRREL

Every fall in Ross County, war was legally declared on small game, which didn't stand a chance against the heavy artillery mounted by the farmer military. Especially squirrel, a favorite target. It got blasted good and stuffed into the back of hunting coats and toted back home, where it was cleaned, fried, and served up crispy autumn-brown on big platters. Particularly at my Aunt Vist's place.

Vist, a vital, warm, cheerful woman, regular churchgoer, and active participant in the Republican Party, loved to cook more than anything, wile away the hours in her steamy kitchen at the back of the Deaton house, preparing her own special country culinary delights.

Here Vistula talks about how small game is fair game. And she imparts detailed instructions for preparing a mess of lip-smacking squirrel.

VISTULA DEATON

The way some people go on 'bout rabbit and squirrel an' quail an' pheasant an' all, you'd think they was human er something. People are just plain crazy anymore. Why, them little creatures was put down on this here earth t' be ate. What else you think they're doin' here?

It's a derned good thing we got huntin' season 'round these parts. If we didn't have, we'd be up t' our ears in rabbits. Them little rascals grow like a house on fire. Throw a couple of 'em in a room overnight an' the next day you got yerself a family. Same with squirrels. Why, them little bucky-toothed devils is all over creation. They're bold little fellas, too, an' gettin' bolder ever year. They eat up ever'thin' in sight. They gnawed right through the side a the granary last spring and did away with half our corn. Wasn't fer huntin' season, this here county would be the squirrel capital of the entire world.

And they're real good eatin', ya know. Yes sir. Nothin' better'n a nice messa squirrel of a cold evening. Nothin' better'n settin' yerself down to a nice messa fresh squirrel and some nice thick squirrel gravy. Good eatin'. Most of 'em are, that is. 'Cept you gotta watch out fer the old ones. They can be tough as pine knots. The young 'uns, them is the best eatin'; the ones that don't weigh much over two pound. An' the red 'uns is best. Grey'uns can get a little gamey. 'Course, you gotta know how to fix 'em.

Whatcha do is clean 'em right away an' eat 'em that same evening. They tend t' toughen up on ya if ya freeze 'em. You gotta get at 'em right away; skin 'em quick and clean 'em fast and get 'em on the table.

The way ya do it is, ya hold 'im in one hand so's 'is belly's face-up. *(Demonstrating.)* Like this here. Then ya take a real sharp knife an' ya stick it right inta 'is throat an' make a cut all the down 'is belly to 'is hind end. See? Cut 'im right down the middle. Then ya grab hold of either side a yer cut an' spread 'im apart so's ya kin grab 'is entrails. Then ya reach in an' grab 'is guts and ya rip 'em right on out. Like this. *(Demonstrating.)* Some of 'em may wanna hang on, so you gotta yank 'em real good. See? After ya clean 'im out, ya take yer knife and ya cut off 'is feet and head. Then ya grab holt of the fur right behind 'is neck an' ya start peelin'. The fur an' skin'll come off slicker'n a whistle. Jus' like peelin' off a rubber glove. But be sure ya git all the fur off. That stuff ever gits in yer throat, you'll be spittin' hair fer a week. Then ya warsh 'im in real cold saltwater so's the meat's real clean and pink-like. Then ya cut 'im up in pieces.

When yer ready t' cook 'im, ya wanna put 'im in a big cast-iron skillet and cover 'im with flower. Then ya cook 'im real easy over a medium fire till 'e's nice an' brown an' tender. Then ya make yer gravy jus' like any other. Then ya serve 'im up.

Nothin' like it. Nothin' like a nice messa squirrel. Sweet eatin'.

A MYSTERY SICKNESS

As far back as anybody could remember, Minnie Ganwer radiated sickness. She had been deathly ill since childhood, suffering daily with aches and pains, dizzy spells, palpitations, complaining of being stricken by the rarest birds of medical exotica. But Minnie always looked wonderful. Her steps were lithe, her cute cherubic face boomed with a roseate glow. But she was always complaining. Always. She was the resident hypochondriac.

Everyone knew that Minnie was in tip-top shape and that her ills were imaginary, but no one ever confronted her with this. Instead, they met her complaints of "terminal colitis" and the never-discovered "tumors big as grapefruits" with sympathetic nods and attendant "ahs" and "ohs." People liked Minnie and just couldn't bring themselves to defeat her with the terrible possibility of good health. And Minnie's hypochondria served her well. It gave her a passel of excuses to avoid real feelings.

MINNIE GANWER

I come real close to gettin' married a couple a times, I did. Was engaged twice, I was.

But, ya know, I've had lots a illness. An' I always seem t' get the sickest when ever I'm havin' a good time. First time somethin' hit me was at this carnival over in Circleville when I was jus' ten years old. I got these awful pains in m' stomach, I 'member. Right down here. *(She presses her fingers to her side dramatically.)* They thought I had 'pendicitis. Had Doc Baker go over me with a fine-tooth comb. But he couldn't find anything wrong. Some doctor.

I had sickness hit me both times I was plannin' to get married, too. The first time I was engaged to a real good-looker; was a government man, in forestry. Made big money. We had our weddin' all set for June. Then, just about a week before the weddin', I took an awful spell where I went all limp and couldn't stop a-twitchin'. Sure threw a monkey wrench inta m' weddin' plans, all right, so I had to call 'em off. I mean, after all, a girl couldn't go off on no honeymoon in the kind a shape I was in, now could she? The second time we were all the way down t' the "I dos" before it hit me. Then, right there in front a all them people, I fell over in a heap and started jerkin' like a grasshopper on a string. Was out cold as a marble for almost an hour. My folks had all kinds a specialists go over me. Even took me up to the Mayo, but nobody could find anything. I wasn't right for weeks. Just sat around in a straight chair lookin' bleary-eyed. Of course, m' fella, he up and took off with a beautician over in Tarlton. Can't say I blamed 'im. Who in their right mind would wanna get saddled with a case like me?

After that, I figured a person with a mystery wedding sickness like me would be a whole lot better off stayin' single. Why, you'd just never know when one of them spells was gonna take ya. Could happen right in the middle o' lovemakin' even. Would be enough to scare a man right out of 'is hair.

Some people is born healthy, some ain't. That's the way it is, I reckon.

PART OF THEIR WORLD

Sarah Detwiler was a slight, attractive, sensitive girl who, after her mother's passing, moved up to Columbus, Ohio, to take a good-paying job with the Columbus Showcase Company. But she returned home frequently to visit her father, her friends, people for whom she had a deep, abiding affection.

This speech, prior to her departure, shortly after her mother's death, reveals how she came to understand the special connection that had existed between her parents.

SARAH DETWILER

We drove out to the grave last Sunday for the first time since the funeral, Dad and I. We didn't talk much. We just drove along real quiet.

It was raining a real fine, soft rain, and the cemetery was real quiet and more pretty and green than I'd ever seen it before. Fact is, I hadn't seen anything like I came to see it that day; or feel things like I felt them, either. It was all kind of like being reborn, or something.

We parked and got out of the car and Dad walked on ahead up to the grave. He walked real careful out of respect for the people buried there. It was like he didn't want to disrupt anything or intrude.

He approached Mom's grave real easy, and when he got there, he just stood over it, looking down at it for a long time with his head bowed and his hat squeezed in his hands real tight.

When I came up alongside of him, he didn't notice. He was still intent on the grave that was still fresh and raised up soft and round. He took the carnations, Mom's favorite, he'd brought along and laid them on the grave gently. Like the way you lay something down late at night when you don't want to wake anyone up. Then he knelt down, still looking at the grave. It was as though he was looking right down into the soul of Mother. And then, right then and there, for the first time, I realized what they'd had between them. A deep love that connected them and still did, even though she'd gone away.

I'd always known they cared a lot for each other, but I'd never felt it like this when she was alive. But now, in death, alluva sudden, I could feel it, what they had between them, and it was beautiful. Alluva sudden I was part of their world.

THEY NEVER KNEW WHAT HIT 'EM

One of my favorite Ross County people was Louise Troxell. Louise, like many people in the area, could lay out a tale with graphic, simplistic, colorful clarity, could make you "see" an event. She was a superb storyteller who enjoyed pulling spellbinding stories from her mixed-bag of anecdotes. One of her favorites had to do with Louise's first cousin, Ray Hicks, a handsome, strapping fellow, lady-killer, and hell-raiser who, during the summer of 1936, purchased a sleek white Indian motorcycle that went like thunder.

I can hear her now—while seated prissily cool under her grape arbor, iced tea at her side, fanning herself with a page from the *Chillicothe Gazette*—laying out in throaty, well-modulated tones the details of cousin Ray's untoward motorcycle adventure.

LOUISE TROXELL

I told Ray, I tried to tell 'im. I said, "Ray, you're gonna git in big trouble on one a them motorsickles." But he wouldn't listen. He always was a real hardhead.

I tried t' tell 'im how dangerous them things were. How ya had t' be careful ridin' 'round on two wheels. Why, a person's gotta have eyes in the back of 'is head t' drive a car even. But a motorsickle? Why, them things is like roller skates with an engine. But, like I said, he wouldn't listen. He had 'is mind set on one a them rascals.

He took me along with 'im t' pick it out; to this here dealer who sold Indian motorsickles over in Kingston. I'll never forget it. He went ahead an' picked himself out a brand-new white Indian with a black buddy seat and a set a saddlebags. Plunked down hard-earned cash for it. Then 'e had 'em put on special mud flaps with red reflectors an' a couple special rear-view mirrors that stuck up about a foot on each handlebar. They looked just like a pair a Mickey Mouse ears a-stickin' up there. It was purty machine, I had to admit. And fast? Whoooooeee! That thing'd git up to a hunderd in a city block.

Now, Ray had always bin a purty wild fella. But once't he got holt a that there motorsickle, he became a wild man. When he climbed up on that machine, he turned inta a regular eedyot. He even got this real funny look on 'im. Like he'd just swallowed a snake, or something. Why, the man would turn inta a wild animal right there before yer eyes.

He tried to git me on that thing more'n once. But no way, brother! I was in no hurry to git to Hades any faster than I was a-goin'. Anyway, the minute after he bought that motorsickle, he jumped on it an' spun gravel all the way outta the dealer's lot till he hit the road. Then, when it grabbed holt of the blacktop, it let out a squeal like a stuck pig and took off right up in the air, ass over applecart. Ray went one way and that machine went the other. Ray rolled along like this big ball of arms and legs and wound up right in the middle of a seed display in front a the hardware store. He carried scabs that made him look like a zebra fer weeks.

But that there spill didn't stop 'im from a-ridin' that thing. No sir. He derned near lived on it all that summer, tearin' 'round like some crazy man. He took m' brother Bob for a ride out on 180, and Bob said he had that motorsickle up t' over a hunderd an' that it was shakin' like a dog on ice. When he got off, 'e swore he'd never git back on one a them things agin. An' Bob was a daredevil.

We all tried t' talk t' Ray. We told 'im that 'e was gonna wind up a-wrappin' that thing around a pole someday. But he wouldn't listen. Then it happened.

It was on a Sund'y, I 'member. Aunt Ida an' Uncle Ory was over. We was all settin' out under the maple tree tryin' to keep cool, eatin' some a George Drum's homemade ice cream. Strawberry, I think it was. We was a-settin' there talkin' hog prices when we heard the explosion. It shook the whole valley, it did. Uncle Ory said, after the sermon they'd heard that morning, he thought maybe it was the end a the world. It sure sounded like it, all right.

Well, what happened is, is that Ray had come over a rise out on Kingston Pike a-goin' better'n ninety, an' on the other side, Harvey Nolan was a-comin' with a truck load a nitro. Understand that that there Indian motorsickle took off a that rise a -lyin' and smacked head-long inta that there truck. Neither Ray er Harvey ever knew what hit 'em—killed 'em both outright. And the explosion blew Ray right out of his shoes. . . . Two-tones, I think they was.

A REAL GOOD DREAM

Vera Shoewalter was strikingly plain. She stood out like a Kansas winter against a sunset sky. She wasn't pretty, she was better than that. She had a stateliness and clean, chiseled features and an effortless way of walking that gave one the illusion she was being blown along. Vera's husband, Gilbert, a railroader, was killed when he fell between trains while working the yard in Circleville. The incident left Vera melancholy, removed, sensitively detached. She lived in a half world, an illusory past tense-world of sequestered childhood days.

VERA SHOEWALTER

When I was just a little girl, Mama an' I usta take long walks up in the hills; usta go out an' walk nearly all day long, we did, just the two of us, all alone, her an' me. Why, we musta traipsed all over these hills one time er other, covered every inch of 'em. I don't think there's a trail up there I haven't bin on. I know these hills, know them well. Sometimes I think I can hear them taling to me of an evening. I can hear their voices oeching across Salt Crick Valley just as plain as anything. Yes, sir, you bet I can. And the hills' voices tell me deep secrets and wonderful stories about the old ways, and about the Indians.

When we walked, Mama usta take long steps, an' it was real hard for me t' keep up with 'er sometimes when the grass an' weeds got high. But when that happened, she'd always stop and wait for me an' take m' hand. And when we'd come t' fences, she usta pick me up real strong-like an' lift me on over t' the other side.

She always talked to me as we walked, too. Talked to me like I was a real person instead of just some little kid. An' she'd tell me stories about the hills an' about the Indian mounds an' the Indians that she made sound real mysterious. An' sometimes her stories would make me scared. But not bad scared, mind you, just good scared like a girl likes t' be scared when 'er mom's nearby an' she knows she can reach out an' touch 'er.

An' sometimes when we walked, she'd put 'er arm around me an' pull me real close an' wool m' head. And this always made me feel special, and warm. An' then she'd look down at me with those big eyes of hers, an' pat me on the shoulder real kind-like and say, "Yer a good girl, Vera, yer a good girl."

MONKEYSHINES

When I was about ten years of age, I accompanied my mother and grandmother on one of their frequent visits to Esther Crabtree's. Esther lived in a big house on Kingston Pike. It was a great house with a long, low roof and a screened-in porch. It was set back from the road among dense willow trees, and it had an air of mystery about it, like it was holding secrets. I remember thinking as we drove up to the place, I wonder if this house is haunted? But it wasn't. Inside it was cheerful and expansive—just like Esther. But the big surprise that day wasn't that the outside of Esther's house belied its interior, it was Esther's chimp, Ray.

Ray was a gift from Esther's brother, Carl Lynchfield, a man of undetermined occupations who traveled widely and returned with all sorts of exotica, the most exotic to date being Ray. And Esther loved the little chimp and gave it free reign over the property. In fact, when we arrived that day, Ray was sitting atop the piano, plucking the petals off a bouquet of zinnias. And during our visit, he availed himself of the room, leaping about randomly as if he were on springs, while Esther filled us in regarding brother Carl:

ESTHER CRABTREE

Carl was always different, ya know. He was never ever like the other kids. He was usually off by himself reading. And he read the darndest things. He had this one book called *Snakes of the Amazon*. He carried it around with him one whole summer. The darn thing scared me half t' death and he knew it, and he used to devil me with it. Sometimes he'd prop it up in a chair next to my bed, so when I woke up, the first thing I'd see was a picture of a Python swallowing a baby pig. Used to scare the living daylights outta me.

Carl was always one for oddities. He kept mice and spiders. He even drug home a three-legged possum once. Said it was better than other possums because it was one leg shy, which made it more valuable. He always went in for the unusual.

His first big trip was to Mexico. When he came back he had a cage full of Armadillos and a new wife—Juanita. Juanita only had one eye and didn't speak English. They stayed with us for a while until Juanita up and ran off with a scissors sharpener. But Carl didn't seem t' be very upset. The only thing that he seemed riled up about was the fact she took the armadillos.

Next he up an' goes to Africa. We got some postal cards from him from places where it took three months for 'em to get here. We couldn't even locate the places in the atlas. Then he started in sending us pictures that showed 'im with half-naked people. And with every picture he sent, *he* got more naked, too. Said he was trying to "go native." Which was okay, we thought, but we just hoped he didn't go so native we couldn't show the pictures to the kiddies.

Just when you'd think he was dead, or something, he'd pop up with a million stories and a trunk loada junk. The last time 'e brought back Ray. He found Ray when 'e was lost in the jungle an' credits the little bugger with saving 'is life. Says that Ray talked to 'im in ape talk and told him how to get back to Buenos Aries.

Now he's off to someplace called Zangbo. It's in Tibet. Said he wants to talk to some kind of high priest, or something.

Ray! Get down off that chandelier!

GOSSIP CENTRAL

The telephone exchange was located in a small building in the center of Hallsville. My father called it "gossip central." It was a small, austere building containing a switchboard with a morass of wires. And it was maintained by the Bacon sisters, Laurie and Rose, who were the conduit for news of births, deaths, sickness, joy—events monumental and trivial. There wasn't much that went on in the community that didn't go through the Bacons.

LAURIE BACON

Last Friday, Luther Maag got a call all the way from Cleveland. From 'is brother who's a foot doctor up there. Understand he makes big money. Them foot specialists charge a fortune to fool with yer toes. Ralph is his name. Was born and raised around here. After high school, he went into feet. Opened up a little office behind Billy Baker's store. Rose went to 'im with bad arches. He told her her feet were ten years older than the rest of 'er body. She told him he was full o' applesauce.

Mae Oates placed a call to her sister, Clara, over in Logan last night. Seems like she's going through hard times and needs t' borrow two hundred dollars. Clara said she was a little short right now, but could spare ten bucks. Mae called her—among other things—a cheap biddy, and hung up the phone on 'er. Can't say that I blame 'er. Everybody knows Clara's got more money than good sense. Her husband up and died last fall and left 'er a feed mill and five hundred acres.

Edith and Bill Crow had a baby boy last week. They wanted a girl. Dan Lambert busted his leg, and they had to rush him to Doc Beaman. He'll be in a cast most of the summer. Freida Hill called up Doris Richter to tell her she burned up her meatloaf. Mary Weiss is going to Cincinnati to visit her sister, Diane, and her husband, Darrell. They live like kings since Darrell got his settlement from the railroad. He fell between cars over in the Circleville switching yard and mangled up his arm—not a pretty sight. The B&O paid off big on it, and now they're comfortable for the rest of their lives. Sometimes a person's best friends are pain an' suffering.

It was a real shock t' everyone when Ruth Stone called from Portsmouth last Sunday a week an' told Donald she wasn't coming home. The poor man was bellowing like a calf. It was almost too hard a conversation to listen in on. Appears she's found a new man—some character who sells kitchen-knife sets. Donald called attorney Black right away and was advised to transfer money as soon as possible.

The Crows finally named their baby, Eugene, after Bill's uncle. He's a roofer an' sider who has a reputation for not showing up because of one too many down at Shady Corners Tavern. We all hope 'is namesake doesn't grow up with a beer habit.

Dan Lambert's leg is a mess, worse than they thought. May have to stick a pin in it.

Clara called Mary Oates back and said she could come up with fifty dollars. Mary spit into the phone receiver. Not very sanitary, but I woulda done the same thing myself.

Looks like Ralph may have twisted one too many tootsies. Called Luther back for money because of some lawsuit or other because he told some woman her feet were ten years older than the rest of her body was and put 'em in plaster casts. Now she's a cripple. Guess that "ten-years-older" business don't work up in Cleveland, either.

Doris Ricther called back Freida Hill and told her to have her oven checked. Darn good advice for any homemaker. Mary Weiss called from Cincy. They went to Coney Island, and she threw up after riding the roller coaster. They visited the botanical gardens and Burger Brewery and later ate out.

Looks like Ruth Stone got mixed up with a real lemon. She called up her sister, Etta, and told 'er that 'er cutlery peddler hasn't sold a knife in over a month. They been eating outta cans. She wants to come on home but doesn't know how t' ask Donald. Etta told 'er to Call Reverend Wormer. She did. Reverend Wormer listened to her sob story, then he called up Donald and told him to transfer money.

Oh, oh—here comes a call in from Cleveland. Could be from Ralph Maag. Maybe he's in more hot water. But, hey, what's it t' me? It's none a my business.

MENFOLK

I LOVE YA, DAD

Eugene Linn's father died during the winter of 1937. A bitter cold winter that sent the mercury to the basement. One evening, shortly after Galen Shaw's passing, my mother and father and I went over to their farm to pay our respects to Eugene and his wife, Clara. It was a solemn trip across the frozen one-lane road that wound through the snow-swept prairie.

At Eugen's place, we all sat in the kitchen, I remember, and the adults spoke in the hushed tones that are reserved for death. Iwas an eerie experience. And Eugene's sadness was deep in him and you could feel it and it made you sad, too.

EUGENE LINN SHAW

Everyone says, "Ya gotta git ahead, ya gotta git ahead." Why, hell, seems like that's all I ever hear anymore. "Ya gotta git ahead." Hell, what is a man, anyway? Just a big old gittin'-ahead machine, a big bunch a nothin' pushin' 'is life through a keyhole? Besides, what's gittin' ahead have t' do with anything, anyhow? With bein' a person, with bein' a man? Heck, my dad was a man. Yer damn right, 'e was. Was 'e ever. He was really somethin'. He was a real pisser, that guy, a real cut off the old plug. Why, he never cared nothin' 'bout gittin' ahead. I don't mean 'e was lazy er nothin' like that, he jus' didn't give a dern fer nobody. He didn't give a hoot if school kept er not. He was his own man, my dad. Yep, he was a real dandy. An' 'e was tougher'n a pine knot, too, that ole devil. Could outwork three men an' a boy. Was a-workin' right up till the day 'e died. He was a good man. An' 'e had a smile bigger'n Ross County.

I sure loved that old man. I loved 'im more'n anything. But I never told 'im so. Damn! I wished I'da told 'im. But 'e always seemed too big and too busy. But I sure loved him, all right. An' 'e loved me, too. Derned right, 'e did. He never ever told me so, but I could tell. You kin feel them things. I sure wish I'da told 'im how I felt about 'im. Damn!

(He looks upward as though looking through the ceiling. His voice rises plaintively as he attempts to reach beyond the grave.) I love ya, Dad! Do ya hear me? I love ya, Dad! I love ya, old man! I love ya, ya old shitkicker! Ya old pisser! Do ya hear me? You were a big man, old man, a helluva man! An' I love ya, Dad, I love ya!

YOU GOTTA DO WHAT YOU GOTTA DO

Of all the locals, none possessed greater energy than tobacco-chewing, expletive-spitting, hard-knocking Kenny Webb. Webb was a hunk of plutonium in forest-green work clothes who radiated industry, was always upbeat, had a zest for living, and a great respect for the job well done. I can see him now, bustling about his kitchen, preparing coffee the consistency of mud, gearing himself for another great Kenny Webb workday.

KENNY WEBB

Damn! Gonna be a cold one t'day. *(Rubbing his hands together briskly.)* Real cold, bet on it. Cold enough t' freeze the horns off a cow out there. An' the roads is gonna be one helluva mess fer sure. An' the tires on the Plymouth is a-wearin' mighty thin, too. I ain't lookin' forward t' that drive t'day, no sir. Not on them highways. Goddammed state won't spend a quarter on the roads. I'm gonna be slidin' all over hell. But, what the hell, a man's gotta do what 'e's gotta do. *(Pouring himself a slug of coffee.)* 'Sides, I got it by the ass. Good job. Good money. An' I look forward to it ever' day.

The way a person gits up in the mornin' says a whole lot about 'im. Says more'n a mouthful anytime. A person's gotta wake up bright an' early t' life; gotta wake up an' take the day by the horns, 'e does; gotta grab holt of it an' shake the bastard real good. 'Cause if ya don't, it's sure gonna wind up a-shakin' him. *(Sips coffee.)* Hell, some people never git their ass in gear. M' brother, fer instance. That there sonofagun ain't got sense enough t' come in outta the rain. Aw, I don't mean 'e's a bad guy er nothin' like that. He jus' ain't got any idee what life's all about. He's kinda movin' through life without a blueprint, ya might say. Know whatta mean? He's a dandy, that guy. *(Sips.)*

An' there's a whole lot jus' like 'im in this here world, too. All runnin' 'round all over the place in all d'rections makin' noise an' makin' busy but never makin' an ounce a sense outta their lives. Way I look at it, a person's gotta git up ever' morning with a plan and grab holt a the day right by the sunbeams. An' when they ain't no sunbeams, well then, 'e's gotta reach way down inside 'imself an' grab a handful a sunshine an' yank 'imself up inta the day. Damn right! *(Sip.)* I know sometimes it ain't all that easy. Hell, no. Not fer me even. Sometimes the thought a hittin' the cold linoleum at five in the mornin' is a real pain. But, what the hell, a person's gotta do what 'e's gotta do.

I got me one helluva job. Machinist. An' the best damned one in that there shop up there, too. You bet on it, buddy! I make that there screw machine set up an' take notice. Ain't no foreman ever found no bugs in my work. No way! Know why? 'Cause I work on tolerances finer'n frog hair, that's why. I turn out them parts right down t' the ten thousandth. When ya do somethin', ya gotta do it right. Too damned many corner cutters these days.

I was the same when it came to farmin', too. Never cut no corners. An' it would a bin easy, too, oh yeah. It woulda bin real easy t' let things slide. 'Cause when yer bossin' yerself, no one else knows the differ'nce. It's real easy when ya gotta foreman a-standin' over ya; then ya gotta mind yer P's and Q's. But when yer on yer own, ya kin slack off 'cause they're ain't no foreman t' kick yer ass. The only foreman ya got then is the one inside yer head. *(Points to his head.)* But he's the Big Foreman . . . this one right up here. He's the one that really counts. He's the one ya can't let down. 'Cause if ya do, why then, brother, yer a-slippin' yerself right inta the grease.

Whatever ya do, ya gotta do it right. Ya gotta jump on it with all fours jus' like a bobcat on a weasel. *(Noting the time.)* Hey! I gotta git outta here!

THE HORSES, THE CORN, AND THE QUIET

Doyle Ruch was a nice guy who lived on the next farm. He was a tall, muscular man with an unruly smile that busted out often all over his tanned, handsome face. He loved farming but was saddled with a city job, a success-oriented wife, and unappreciative in-laws who leaned on him for support. When Doyle spoke of the land, of farming, his eyes buzzed with delight, and that big unruly smile would devour his face. Here he reflects on happier times:

DOYLE RUCH

On real cold mornin's, I usta harness up the team 'fore I led 'em down t' the pound fer a drink. I 'member the harness usta be all frozen an' stiff an' hard t' bend. M' hands usta git colder'n hell. Damn canvass gloves never did keep yer hands warm. By the time I got through a-bucklin' that frozen harness, m' hands'd be achin' an' numb. I usta beat 'em an' blow on 'em an' even cuss the bastards. But it didn't do no good.

The horses could feel the cold, too. They'd be s' cold they wouldn't even move. They'd jus' stand there a-lookin' straight ahead with big frosty breaths a-comin' outta their snoots. Poor goddamned horses, they didn't wanna go noplace. You could tell what they was athinkin'. "Dumb sonofabitch. What the hell's 'e wanna go out in them fields t'day for? Jus' look at 'im. Beatin' 'is hands and stompin' 'round like some eedyot. He oughtta be up at the house settin' in the kitchen where it's warm."

After I got the team harnessed, I usta lead 'em on down t' the pond behind the springhouse. I 'member how the waygon tracks an' the horses' hoof prints usta freeze over, an' ya had t' walk real careful fer fear a fallin' on yer breakfast. The horseshit even froze up, too, an' lay in the road like big iron balls. It's a good thing, frozen horseshit, 'cause frozen horseshit don't stink.

When I got the horses t' the pond, I usta bust a hole in the ice so they could drink. After they'd finished drinkin', I'd lead 'em on back t' the barn an' hitch 'em up t' the ole green waygon. An' when they was hitched, I'd lead 'em on out to the fields t' load up the corn that'd been piled up next t' the shocks. I'd pull the waygon up next t' the piles an' then git down an' scoop up the corn inta the waygon. I'd scoop away till the cold didn't bother me no more. An' after I'd been a-scoopin' fer awhile, nothin' bothered me, nothin'. There was jus' me, them horses, the corn, an' the quiet.

SHE WAS A PURTY LITTLE THING

Joe Clark ran one of the two general stores in Hallsville, Ohio. The other was run by Billy Baker whose place was just up highway 180. Joe had kind eyes and a memorable head of thick white hair. He was also a Democrat to the core. I mention his politics because most of the community was Republican and, therefore, those embracing the Donkey were glaring anomalies. Joe's store was neat and rustic and smelled good. It was also stocked to the roof with a wide variety of merchandise.

Going to Joe's store was always a major event in my life because I loved to browse it and make exciting discoveries and ogle the knife display. And Joe would slip me candy and on occasion slice me a nice fat wedge from a great golden moon of longhorn cheese.

Joe was a nice man and everybody in the community spoke highly of him. And he had never married due to a tragedy that had left irrevocable scars. He had never married because of the loss of "a purty little thing."

JOE CLARK

Yes sir, she was sure a purty little thing. Her name was Martha and she lived over near Kingston. She was somethin'. Purty ain't the word for 'er. In fact, I don't think there's a word-spinner on the face o' the earth who could describe her with justice. And she was nice an' sweet an' 'er skin was just as soft as a cow's ear, it was. An' she usta treat me just like the king a the world; made me feel special. An' she sure wasn't out after me for my money, either, that's fer sure. Heck, I was workin' at the feed mill then, pullin' down nothin' but debts. M' clothes was patches on patches. I had me this old car that was all rusted out. I was in one heckuva shape. But she still loved me; she sure did, all right.

She usta come meet me every night after work at the mill. Every night, rain 'er shine, she never missed. I can just see 'er now, comin' up the road with 'er long hair flyin', 'er heels a-kickin' up sparks on the asphalt. Then one night after work I seen her comin' just like as usual; a-comin' along the roadway a-smilin' and tossin' 'er head just like always. And then, God knows why she did it, she stepped out on the highway without lookin'; stepped right out in front of a high-ballin' semi, she did. The guy couldn't stop. Wasn't his fault. She didn't give 'im a chance. Killed 'er outright.

She sure was was a purty little thing.

YOUR FAMILY'S ALL YOU'VE GOT

Icouldn't resist putting in one of my father's philosophical out-pourings; one of his frequent, evangelical ramblings that he presented dramatically, with flamboyant, sweeping gestures. Dad's speeches were kind of like hillbilly sonatas. They embraced earthy themes, which were developed with a counterpoint of profanities and recapitulated with verve and correlative verbal thunder. The scene: The kitchen on a winter's eve. Dad is sitting over coffee nursing a Chesterfield, watching the women do the dishes. He leans back casually in his chair, rolls his tongue around inside his mouth with a thoughtful, cheek-bulging revolution, levels his cigarette at me instructively, and begins:

NOBLE KARSHNER

Skipper Jack, yer fam'ly's all ya got, boy. An' don't ya ever forgit it. An' don't ever let it go an' git weak on ya; don't ever let anythin' tear it apart. 'Cause yer fam'ly's yer foundation, the thing ya can always lean on when the goin' gits rough. An' it'll git rough sometimes, too, oh yea. Rougher'n a cob. Lemme guarantee ya, yer gonna have some days when ya think they ain't gonna be no tomarra. Days when there ain't anything but a big bunch a fog settin' over yer head. An' them is the days when yer fam'ly's gonna mean somethin' special to ya, when they're gonna be a rock for ya to hold on to. A person's fam'ly's real important. *(He takes a drag on his cigarette.)*

But it ain't always gonna be easy t' hold on to an' hold together. No siree. Sometimes you'll git t' the place where ya wanna blow the whole shootin' match sky high. Jus' like 'round here, fer instance. Sometimes I'd like t' take that brother-in-law a mine an' shake 'im real good. An' that wife a his with her bitchin' and complainin' all the time. Why, even yer mom here, she even gits me a little edgy sometimes, too. But, what the hell, that's life. Hell, ever'one gits under yer skin once't in a while. After all . . . ain't nobody perfect. *(With a broad wink.)* 'Cept mebbe yer old man, that is. *(He flicks an ash into his pants cuff.)*

But ya can't let a little problem, a little blow up, git in the way, upset the fam'ly. Ain't worth it 'cause ya lose too much. Ya gotta be careful not t' let little things drive a wedge ya can't pry out. Yep, yer foundation, that's what a fam'ly is. A foundation that gives ya a right angle on life, that keeps ya from a goin' off an' burnin' out like a Roman candle in midair. *(He looks about him.)* Take this here farmhouse, fer instance. It's gotta real foundation under it that makes it solid as a goddamned rock. Jus' like the people who built it. They was solid, too. Yep, they built this here place to last. Why, this here sonofabitch'll stand forever. You ever see the joists under this place? Why, they're tree trunks, hand hewn, this big around. . . . *(He forms his arms in a manner indicting the large diameter of the logs.)* The goddamned Pennsylvania Dutch bastards that hung this place together knew what the hell they was a-doin', knew how t' paste a place together. An' they knew how t' keep glue on the fam'ly ties, too. 'Cause they knew damned well if that there ever busted, they was gonna be in real trouble. *(He reflects.)*

My folks, yer grandfolks, they never had nothin' far as money was concerned. Poor as hell, they was. But they always made us kids feel good an' safe 'cause they made us feel solid. We had the foundation, like I said. An' they was always there when we needed 'em. They wasn't off a-galavantin' somewhere, they was home with us. That's the big secret of child-raisin' . . . *bein' there!* Ya gotta be there. Come supper time, a man's feet should be under 'is own table, not under the table of a rester'nt somewhere. Bein' there. Them's the two most important words when it comes t' bringin' up kiddies. 'Cause if a child don't git no raisin' he's gonna wind up raisin' hell.

Yep, we had the foundation, all right. Even when Mom died an' us kids had t' go off t' foster homes for a while, we was still solid, still had the feelin' a fam'ly between us. That's 'cause we had the foundation in our heads. So remember, boy, when the chips is down, the fam'ly counts. *(He grinds out his smoke and stands quickly.)*

Now, c'mon, I wanna take ya down in the cellar an' show ya them joists. *(Again he demonstrates the large diameter of the logs with his arms.)* This big around! You'll see!

MR. BLOOD

About a mile outside town, a small, weathered building sat cupped in the palm of a long valley. Smoke the consistency of steel slime oozed from its chimney and drifted off laboriously in black, unhappy, pendulous globs. These moody, cloudy wads were the by-product of boiling viscera being stirred with casual professionalism by Bert Strange. Bert, or Mr. Blood as he was referred to by the locals, was the proprietor of the slaughterhouse. He was a jolly good fellow, toothless, muscularly squat, and happy as a fly in cream as he went about his rendering.

Bert's apron out-Pollocked Jackson Pollock with its overlapping complexity of blood drippings, hand wipings, knife cleanings, and gut slops. Bert was an unsavory, rotten sight, and perpetually redolent of decayed animal carcasses even after vigorous scrubbings with the most pungently scented soap sold by the Watkins Man. You always knew when Bert Strange was in the room.

Bert loved his work, viewed it as a practical matter, found in it no repulsiveness, and had little tolerance for squeamishness in the presence of blood.

BERT STRANGE

Most people are downright silly when it comes to a little blood. Why hell, ain't nothin' wrong with blood. There ain't nothin' wrong with it a-tall. Blood's real. If we didn't have it in us, we'd be in one heckuva fix, all of us.

I 'member my grandaddy usta drink a pint a warm blood ever' day fer years. He usta go down t' the slaughterhouse after they'd stuck a bull an' git a bucket full a that there fresh blood. Then he'd drink it straight down jus' like he was chuggin' a milkshake. Nothin' to it. Slick as a whistle. Why, you shoulda seen that man. The picture a health, 'e was. It was that blood, no doubt about it. It kept iron in 'im. A person's gotta have lotsa iron in 'is system. An' maybe a trace a alcohol, too. Keeps the juice a-flowin'.

Hell, blood's the red river a life, the God-sent gift to our veins. A wonderful thing. Funny how people are scared of it. No reason. It's real. Part a life. Hell . . . it *is* life! I guess people jus' can't face up t' the real side a livin'. They're always runnin' from what's jus' plain an' natural in this here world. Why, blood an' guts ain't no big deal, not a-tall. Why can't folks jus' face up t' what's inside? Why, what's on the inside is jus' as important as what's on the out. More important, come t' think of it. Lemme ask ya: What would ya rather have, anyway . . . yer heart er yer hair?

It's what's inside, what's down deep that makes a person tick, that gives 'im beauty and health. If a man's sick on the inside, either in 'is guts or 'is head, then he's gotta real problem. Outside don't mean nothin'. Take yer Abe Lincoln, fer instance. He was a heck of a lookin' thing. But inside, mister, inside he had it workin' fer 'im, had all his machinery a-runnin' on greased wheels. How many people look real good on the outside but on the inside they ain't worth a damn? Plenty, bet on it. I sure know a bunch of 'em, that's fer sure.

Everthing owes its existence t' what's on the inside. Go ahead an' bust open a milkweed sometime, fer instance. Know what ya git? Ya git a whole bunch a milky stuff all over yer fingers. An' that there milky stuff is the lifeblood a that there plant. It's the juice that keeps it a-humpin'. Bust open a person er animal an' ya git red juice. Same thing. Jus' a different color, that's all.

I know that that there bull's blood sure kept grandpa goin' fer years. Even in 'is old age he had skin jus' as smooth as a melon. Hell, t'day people got spider-web faces 'fore they're thirty-five. But grandpa had a baby-butt skin on 'im right up t' the day he had 'is stroke at ninety-two. He got down out in the granary, I 'member. We found 'im a-layin' there mumblin' crazy stuff an' lookin' all bleary-eyed.

He was a vegetable fer a long time after that. Didn't have any control over his vital organs. But every now an' then he'd have these periods where he got better an' it looked like he was gonna snap outta it. He lived t' be a hundered an' one. I gotta feeling it was all that there bull's blood inside 'im.

IDYLL TO BEER

Dude Henderson was a fireplug of a man with thick wrists and stubby, powerful, work-worn hands. He was noted for being able to hold a nine-pound sledge at arm's length and lift a bar stool from one leg. Dude was a neat guy for a kid to know. Because he never made you feel like a kid. He made you feel grown-up and important. When he did chores around the farm, he allowed me to work right alongside of him. Hell, he trusted me. If more adults understood this, there would be far fewer prescriptions for Valium. Dude was also noted for being a handyman par excellence who could, as my dad used to say, "Do anything." But the thing he preferred doing more than anything was hang out at Shady Corners Tavern in Adelphi and guzzle beer, a beverage he ingested voluminously, while sitting around "The Corners" bullshitting with the boys. Here, Dude waxes poetic regarding his favorite libation:

DUDE HENDERSON

(*Examining the bottle of beer in his hand as if it were the Hope diamond.*) Beer. Beer. Why hell, beer's the best damned drink in the world. An' it's honest lookin', just like it tastes. (*Admiring the brew.*) Jus' look at it. Prettier'n a woman in a sweater without underwear. Yer damned tootin'.

Hell, I sure usta put away the beer in the old days. Back when I could bite a pine knot out of a two-by-four. I usta really per 'er away. Damn right! Usta drink beer till m' bladder felt like a-bustin' an' m' belly swelled up like a toad's. Usta drink an' piss, piss an' drink. Drink one an' piss two. I usta piss streams a beer s' damn pure it shoulda been bottled back up an' drank all over again.

I 'member some nights me an' some a the other guys usta git about half tight an' hold pissin' contests t' see which one a us could let 'er fly the farthest. One time ole Vemont Pearson put 'er almost twenty foot.

An' sometimes in the wintertime a whole buncha us usta git all pissed up an' try an' write our names an' cuss words in the snow. I 'member one night around the holidays when Jerry Congrove had enough pee stored up in 'im t' write "Merry Christmas an' a Happy New Year." Looked real purty, too. An' 'e did it standin' in a second-story winda.

Beer! Nothin' like it. Nothin at all. Best damn drink there was an' ever will be.

A SCARY SITUATION

He used to sit in front of Billy Baker's general store on a long weathered bench that advertised Hill Brothers' Funeral Home in Kingston. He'd relax there, weather permitting, chewing the juicy stub of an unlit cigar, unwinding tales that were balloon-sized, apocryphal, fanciful, thoroughly arresting, and ones he swore were— "On the Holy Bible may God strike me dead"—true.

Valentine was a local floater who did odd jobs. But most of the time he was luxuriating on his bench, head back and over to one side as though he were listening. Which he wasn't, because he was always talking away from the side of his mouth that wasn't encumbered by a saliva-ripe R. G. Dunn.

VALENTINE WALDMAN

Hey, you talk about yer scary situations. Lemme tell ya 'bout the time me, m' brother Bob, an' Vemont was out a-coon huntin'.

It was in the fall of the year, it was, an' the leaves was just about all offa the trees. It was one a them damp, cold nights that reached down an' grabbed ya inside yer clothes an' took holt a yer soul.

Well, anyway, the three a us was a-hunchin' down like three soggy bears in the middle a the old maple grove over near Laurelville. An' all around us there was this big city a maples a-shootin' up outta the ground straight at heaven like a bunch a skeletons a-reachin' up fer salvation. Must a bin ten thousand trees in that there grove, maybe even twenty!

Anyway, here we was a-settin' there when, alluva sudden like, we see these here little teeny-weeny-bitty lights a-way off in the night across Salt Crick Valley. Like pin-dots they was, a-shimmerin' along like some kind a fire-fairies on top a the ground. 'Cept they didn't seem t' be on the ground, not really. They seemed more like they was a-floatin' along in midair.

Now, us boys looked at each other with eyes bigger'n heifers'. We didn't know what was goin' on. Mebbe we was a-settin' on the outskirts a hell lookin' inta the eternal furnace. Mebbe it was the end a the world! Coulda bin. We didn't know.

Well sir, we blew out the kerosene lantern we was carryin' an' set there in the misty dark real quiet-like, a-watchin' them there silver dots a-comin' closer an' closer. Jus' like an army a fiery devils, they was. Eyes outta hell, they was. Eyes outta hell! An' they kept on a-comin', advancin'. Faster an' faster like they was closin' in fer the kill!

We all dropped down on the ground an' laid there sayin' private prayers in the wet leaves. An' them hell-eyes kept on a-comin', movin' in on us, closer an' closer till they was right above us on a little rise above the maple grove. And then, then we finally seen what them blazin' night-eyes was.

They was an army a KKKs all dressed up in their white sheets. An' each one a them was a-carryin' a torch. Hell, there musta bin a thousand of 'em, at least. So many of 'em we could feel the heat from their torches burnin' through the night. Then, this here army a burnin' ghosts made this big circle. An' then a bunch of 'em come inta the middle a the circle with a cross that musta bin at least two stories high. An' then they stuck the cross in the ground an' lit it on fire an' it went up in flames like—whoosh!—a-bustin' a glare a light over the whole county. An' we didn't dare move, any of us. No sir. 'Cause we knew that them there white-sheeted bastards didn't take kindly to uninvited guests.

Then I thought, Hell, we don't have t' take this here crap! What the hell we layin' here shiverin' like a bunch a wet dogs for, anyway? So I says t' Bob an' Vemont, I says, "We don't have t' put up with this crap. What the hell we doin', anyway? Hell, we're Americans, first-class, grade-A members a the Land a the Free! We'll show them bastards! We'll git up an' walk right inta the middle of 'em an' blow our noses on their goddamn sheets! Whaddaya say, boys?"

Well sir, we all looked at each other, then we all stood up. Yes sir, damned right. We all stood up and then . . . then we all run t' beat hell!

A REAL LIVE QUOTA BUSTER

The community had one eating place—a one-room affair situated between the telephone exchange and Jerry Congrove's garage. It was a downbeat joint containing nondescript tables and chairs and three or four unstable stools facing a greasy grill where proprietor Estil Good prepared cheeseburgers of top-grade beef that were the best thing you ever teethed into. Estil was tall and lanky and detached and moved very slowly. He reminded me of a stoned flamingo.

At one time Estil had been offered a sales position, but—like so many to whom opportunity is a threat—had vacillated and, as a consequence, became a slave to his two-bit grease factory. Here he reflects upon what might have been:

ESTIL GOOD

One time I was gonna give up this here greaseball. Damn right! Was gonna go on up t' Cleveland an' become a salesman. Yep, I was gonna be a real live quota buster, I was, closin' the big 'uns, makin' the big money, livin' high off the hog. I coulda bin the hottest-shot salesman ever t' open up 'is catalog on the counters of America. I had it in me. I had the stuff, yer damn right I did. I was a born peddler. *(He reflects, then goes off into a fantasy sales pitch.)*

"Hello there, Mr. Buyer, how ya bin? How's the weather bin? Lotsa rain? No kiddin'? Why, we ain't had hardly any rain up in New York this year. Just moderatin'." An' then he'd say, "New York, Estil? Why, I didn't know you was livin' up in New York. Lordy." An' then I'd say, "Oh yeah, I bin up there ever since they made me Vice President a the company way back last spring." And he'd say.,"Vice President. I'll be derned. Boy, you're sure somethin', Estil. Tell ya what. Jus' go ahead an' write me up fer ever'thing in yer catalog, okay?" *(He reflects for a spell and then returns to reality.)*

But, what the heck, all that travlin', runnin' 'round all over the place. No way fer a man t' live. At least here I got me security, a warm bed ever' night. I coulda had the job, though, oh yeah, damned right I coulda. *(Beat.)* But I jus' couldn't seem t' break outta this here one-horse place. Somethin' kept me from a-goin'. The life wasn't fer me, I guess. Lotsa fellas go fer that kind a life, though. They love runnin' 'round all over. One hotel after another. Livin' outta a suitcase. An' they make big money, too. An' women. . . . *(He reflects for a moment on all the beauties out there on "the road," then snaps back.)* But, they's a bunch a dopes. I'll bet most of 'em would like t' have a stake in a nice little business like this here. *(A long reflection.)* I often wonder, though. Often wonder what kind a salesman I woulda made. I bet I coulda cracked the big 'uns an' made me a bundle. Prob'ly coulda made me a fortune.

THE LAND'S LIKE A WOMAN

When I was growing up back in rural Ohio, I don't remember hearing about ecology, never heard the word even. But it seemed like everybody practiced it. Every farmer was keenly aware of the balance of nature, practiced conservation, was discreet, judicial in his treatment of the land and wildlife. Especially Dorsey Mohler.

Dorsey lived ascetically on a small farm up in Fox Hollow. A naturalist, he knew the Latin name for every plant and tree in the county and was, despite the fact that he was virtually uneducated, well-schooled regarding ecological matters and boomingly vocal about the "damned fools who spit in the eye of nature."

Dorsey was a seemingly indestructible sort who wore nothing but a T-shirt most of the year and scoffed at the weaklings who wrapped themselves in protective garments. He faced life and the elements with happy tenacity, living off nuts and berries, stomping about his property with an air of triumphant independence, his unfashionably long gray hair churning about his weathered, leonine, Germanic head.

DORSEY MOHLER

Ya know, there just ain't nothin' as good as workin' the land; nothin' quite as satisfyin' as comin' t' grips with nature.

Know what? When ya think about it, the land's a whole lot like a woman. Yep, like a woman. She's got a lotta moods, a lotta mystery, an' she's beautiful. Yeah, beautiful. Like when the sun comes bustin' up over 'er of a-morning makin' 'er nice and soft-like. Then she takes on a whole bunch a gold jewelry an' begins a-glintin' over the new day. An' when it rains, when it rains she lays there real sad like with big puddles a tears in 'er eyes. An' the snow, the snow turns 'er inta an ice cube and she don't want nothin' t' do with ya fer a while.

An' the land, just like a woman, can make ya love 'er er make ya mad as hell. An' I'll tell ya, it takes a real man t' go ahead an' love 'er with ever'thin' 'e's got in 'im when she's a-goin' through 'er moods. An' the land, jus' like a woman, ya gotta make love to real easy. An' then, after yer done, ya gotta let 'er rest up fer a while, let 'er take a little nap before the next go 'round. An' if ya treat 'er right, if ya give 'er respect, she'll never let ya down.

(He reaches down and scoops up a handful of earth, examines it, smells it.) Ya know, this here Ross County land's the best. It's rich! Just like a great big hunk a chocolate pie settin' right here in the middle o' southern Ohio. The crops that come outta this part a the country is as fine as they is in the world. An' ya know why? Ya know why? 'Cause the farmers 'round here treat it right, that's why, like they do their women. They're gentle and don't abuse.

SHOES

John Crider went with my aunt, Ruth, for nearly fifteen years. They were, according the best of my recollection, engaged for nearly this amount of time, too. Until Ruth got tired of John's procrastinating. Even though long engagements were more or less the vogue in those days, I guess Ruth figured that fifteen years was a little excessive.

I remember John as a man of heavily starched shirts and highly shined shoes. Grandma used to say that John looked like wax—which meant fastidious. He sure looked like wax to me. Nothing was out of place, and his clothes were well-tailored and snappy. John was dapper.

John ran a shoe store in Logan, and he spoke often and passionately about shoes and the shoe business. Shoes were his life. He loved shoes. When he'd talk of insteps and vamps and styles and hard-to-fit customers, his eyes widened perceptively.

JOHN CRIDER

A shoe tells you a whole lot about a person. It's a regular road map t' their soul. You can figure out all about a person by studyin' 'is feet. Take your narra foot, for instance. A narra foot tells you a person has artistic ways. They either write poetry or paint or play a musical instrument, or something. I call these kinda feet "restless feet." Because people with artistic ways tend to be unsettled. Like Dana Slade. She was a seven double-A with a quad heel. A foot on her like a banana. I got her for an artistic type from the moment I slipped a William Greene mule on her foot. I said to myself, This here is one restless person. And I was sure enough right on the money. She ran off with that advance man for Pathe Pictures. Show business.

Now your person with wide feet is a whole different story. Wide-feet people are solid like the foundation they're standing on. They are also slow and usually boring. Like Sam Cunningham. Here is your typical twelve double-E. A solid citizen. Why, he's been an Elk for forty years. Nice fella. But the man's so slow, he's two days behind yesterday. And he could bore the stink off a hog. I sat next to him at the last Elk's picnic, and 'e spent the whole time talking about Mammoth Cave, Kentucky. He had all the dimensions and all the stuff about how it was formed way back when men were monkeys. And he wonders why Doris left him. Your typical double-E.

Now, when you come across a wide/short foot, you've got a case for Ripley. I once had this woman come in with a four-D. Looked like she was wearing building blocks. I don't know how she stood up. And she was the meanest person I ever met before or since. And it didn't take a magician to figure out why. Heck, she was living an off-balance life. You can't go teetering through life on little cubes an' expect t' be pleasant. When I told 'er I couldn't fit 'er, she spit at me. Spit at me! You gotta watch out for your short-and-wides.

We gotta whole bunch o' new models coming in next month. Latest outta the northeast. Finest leather, and latest styles. I can't wait to get those babies in my store window. They won't last a week. Remember those two-tone oxfords I got in last spring? Why, I sold them so fast my shoehorn almost caught on fire. People love smart shoes. Shoes. They're necessary, practical, and a new pair makes a person feel like money in a fireproof safe.

RHYTHM KING

The only dance orchestra to play around Ross County was led by Ed Zissler. Ed was a spirited fellow and conducted his outfit with verve and panache. He was a drummer and led the band from behind a set of archaic Leedys that were accessorized by a red, Chinese tomtom and an auspicious-looking row of temple blocks. The temple blocks were brightly painted, gourd-like percussive instruments that emitted a sound close to that of horses hooves' on wet pavement. I really loved it when Ed whacked his temple blocks because they lent an air of buoyancy to the music. Ed was a fine drummer. He had a great sense of time and played with flourish and enthusiasm. Ed just didn't play the drums—he was part of them.

ED ZISSLER

I first started out in music with the accordion—a Wurlitzer. It was black and had ivory bass buttons. My name, Eddie, was spelled out in silver sparkle along the side of the keyboard. When I played, the silver usta flash an darn near knock the eyes outta people. My big number was "Lady o' Spain," and I usta play it for thunder. I wore a white silk shirt with floppy sleeves. When I'd go into double time, I'd fling my hair around and make a buncha funny faces. People would go wild and clap and stomp their feet. I guess ya might say I was flashy.

But I never liked the accordion. I always felt like some kinda simp playin' the darn thing. The instrument was my mother's idea. She'd seen this guy in a traveling tent-show playing one and she decided that the squeeze-box was for me. So, she talked Dad into buying one and started me in on lessons with Frank Corelli, a slick little Italian fella who had a smile like Dutch Cleanser. I took lessons for almost three years, and the only tune I ever got right was "Lady o' Spain." All accordion players had to learn it—it was a must. But most learn other songs, too. But not me. I fell down on the Strauss waltzes, Victor Herbert, Romberg—you name it. I could never figure out the left hand for anything but "Lady o' Spain." My fingers played in the cracks for everything else. But I sure as heck could play the daylights outta "Lady."

I saw my first drum set in the window of Summers an' Sons in Chillicothe. Summers and Sons was the big-deal music store in the county, and they advertised on the side of barns with snappy stuff like, "Teach a Boy to Blow a Horn, and He'll Never Blow a Safe." Summers an' Sons was way ahead when it came to outdoor advertising. I knew right away that the drums were for me, so I talked Mom inta trading the Wurlitzer for an' old bass drum an' a beat-up snare. Was the best move I ever made. Drums for me was a real natural. Why, even after a half-dozen lessons, I was playin' a pretty decent roll.

In high school, I was the star of the marching band and even won a drummers' contest up in Columbus. My sticks moved so fast when I played "The Three Camps," one of the judges wondered why I didn't get splinters.

I woulda gone on t' the big time, but when my dad came down with cancer, I figured I'd better help out 'round the farm. But I kept on drumming, and eventually organized the Ross County Stompers. We play all the music jobs in the area—the weddings, proms, college dances, and the like. We have a good reputation, and people come from all over t' hear us. There's this one kid who comes to all our engagements. He goes nuts when I play the temple blocks.

ORDER DIRECT

MONOLOGUES THEY HAVEN'T HEARD, Karshner. Modern speeches written in the language of today. $7.95.

MORE MONOLOGUES THEY HAVEN'T HEARD, Karshner. More exciting living-language speeches. $7.95.

SCENES THEY HAVEN'T SEEN, Karshner. Modern scenes for men and women. $7.95.

FOR WOMEN, MONOLOGUES THEY HAVEN'T HEARD, Pomerance. Contemporary speeches for actresses. $7.95

MONOLOGUES FOR KIDS, Roddy. 28 wonderful speeches for boys and girls. $7.95.

MORE MONOLOGUES for KIDS, Roddy. More great speeches for boys and girls. $7.95.

SCENES FOR KIDS, Roddy. 30 scenes for girls and boys. $7.95.

MONOLOGUES FOR TEENAGERS, Karshner. Contemporary teen speeches. $7.95.

SCENES FOR TEENAGERS, Karshner. Scenes for today's teen boys and girls. $7.95.

HIGH SCHOOL MONOLOGUES THEY HAVEN'T HEARD, Karshner. Contemporary speeches for high schoolers, $7.95.

DOWN-HOME, Karshner. Speeches for men and women in the language of rural America. $7.95.

MONOLOGUES FROM THE CLASSICS, ed. Karshner. Speeches from Shakespeare, Marlowe and others. An excellent collection for men and women, $7.95.

SCENES FROM THE CLASSICS, ed. Maag. Scenes from Shakespeare and others. $7.95.

SHAKESPEARE'S MONOLOGUES THEY HAVEN'T HEARD, ed. Dotterer. Lesser known speeches from The Bard. $7.95.

MONOLOGUES FROM CHEKHOV, trans. Cartwright. Modern translations from Chekhov's major plays: *Cherry Orchard, Uncle Vanya, Three Sisters, The Sea Gull.* $7.95.

MONOLOGUES FROM GEORGE BERNARD SHAW, ed. Michaels. Great speeches for men and women from the works of G.B.S. $7.95.

MONOLOGUES FROM OSCAR WILDE, ed. Michaels. The best of Wilde's urbane, dramatic writing from his greatest plays. For men and women. $7.95.

WOMAN, Susan Pomerance. Monologues for actresses. $7.95.

WORKING CLASS MONOLOGUES, Karshner. Speeches from blue collar occupations. Waitress, cleaning lady, policewoman, truck driver, miner, etc. $7.95.

MODERN SCENES FOR WOMEN, Pomerance. Scenes for today's actresses. $7.95.

MONOLOGUES FROM MOLIERE, trans. Dotterer. A definitive collection of speeches from the French Master. The first translation into English prose. $7.95.

SHAKESPEARE'S MONOLOGUES FOR WOMEN, trans. Dotterer. $7.95.

DIALECT MONOLOGUES, Karshner/Stern.13 essential dialects applied to contemporary monologues. Book and Cassette Tape. $19.95.

YOU SAID A MOUTHFUL, Karshner. Tongue twisters galore. Great exercises for actors, singers, public speakers. Fun for everyone. $7.95.

TEENAGE MOUTH, Karshner. Modern monologues for young men and women. $7.95.

SHAKESPEARE'S LADIES, Dotterer. A second book of Shakespeare's monologues for women. With a descriptive text on acting Shakespeare. $7.95.

BETH HENLEY:MONOLOGUES FOR WOMEN, Henley.*Crimes of the Heart* and others. $7.95.

CITY WOMEN, Smith. 20 powerful, urban monologues. Great audition pieces. $7.95.

KIDS' STUFF, Roddy. 30 great audition pieces for children. $7.95.

KNAVES, KNIGHTS, and KINGS, Dotterer. Speeches for men from Shakespeare. $8.95.

DIALECT MONOLOUES, VOL II, Karshner/Stern. 14 more important dialects. Farsi, Afrikaans, Asian Indian, etc. Book and Cassette tape. $19.95.

RED LICORICE, Tippit. 31 great scene-monologues for preteens. $7.95.

MODERN MONOLOGUES for MODERN KIDS, Mauro. $7.95.

SPEECHES & SCENES from OSCAR'S BEST FILMS. Dotterer. $19.95.
